Say A Little Prayer

LaWanna Harrod

© 2015 LaWanna Harrod

All rights reserved. No part of this publication may be reproduced, distributed, or transmitted in any form or by any means, including photocopying, recording, or other electronic or mechanical methods, without the prior written permission of the publisher, except in the case of brief quotations embodied in critical reviews and certain other noncommercial uses permitted by copyright law. For permission requests, email the publisher, addressed "Attention: Permissions Coordinator," at the email address below.

Harrod Enterprises
Clinton, MD 20735
www.harrodpublishing.com

All Scriptures, unless otherwise noted are from the *New International, New King James* and the *Message* versions of the Bible. Bible Gateway, a division of The Zondervan Corporation, 3900 Sparks Drive SE, Grand Rapids, MI 49546 USA.

Say A Little Prayer   ISBN: 978-0-9960763-4-0

FOREWORD

When we pray, it is our lifeline to God. It is our opportunity to get God's attention and in turn, give Him our devotion. Prayer allows us to cease what we are doing and focus on spending intimate moments with God. It is our line of communication with God that impacts our lives and the lives of those who are connected to us.

The power of prayer can change your destiny if you allow it. Indeed, prayer is God's method of communication and confirmation to many issues that we may face in life. Every believer should take time to pray each day and give God room to work on and in them. The application of prayer is not just another task for the believer to complete; rather, it is a necessity for longevity in this Christian race.

It is my desire that you would allow God to speak to you through every prayer and declaration that embodies this book. Permit God to change your old habits and watch Him transform your life through the words that you put into the atmosphere.

As you are changed through the power of prayer, let God do something new within you. Unleash the power of prayer to bring deliverance to yourself and to the nations. Allow God to birth new ideas and creative thoughts that will bring you into your next ministry assignment, change your spiritual appetite and strengthen you to walk into destiny.

The compilation of short prayers and declarations in this book will have a lasting impact on your life. Reading this will grant a refreshing in your life as you are transformed by the renewing of you mind. Ultimately, your renewed mind will allow you to confront and conquer the challenges of the daily hustle and bustle of life. When you pray, do so with confidence that is integrated with faith. The word of God reminds us in Hebrews 4:16 (KJV) *"Let us therefore come boldly unto the throne of grace that we may obtain mercy, and find grace to help in time of need."*

I am reminded of an old song written by Benjamin Cureton that instructs us to, "whisper a prayer in the morning, whisper a prayer at noon, whisper a prayer in the evening; it will keep your heart in tune."

Pastor Myron K. Leach
Shiloh Abundant Life Church North
Forestville, Maryland

PRAYERS

"Father, give us a deeper hunger for your WORD! Let us eat and be delighted as you reveal more of who you are and what you have purposed us to be; vessels full of your Glory."

I pray blessings upon your life according to Numbers 6:22-27,

God's protection
"The Lord bless you and keep you"

God's favor
"The Lord make His face shine upon you"

God's grace
"and be gracious to you"

God's peace
"The Lord turn His Face towards you and give you peace," in Jesus Name.

Holy Spirit, help me to see and remember that my life is a gift. Since this new day is filled with potential, help me to be kind, gentle and patient with others. Teach me to see the things that I often ignore and help me to tune in carefully to your voice. I declare that no traps, accidents or mishaps will penetrate my day. I stand with the expectation that something good is headed my way. I praise you, good health, wealth and every provision that you have in store for me. Thank you for the blessings that you will bestow upon my family, pastors and friends. You are worthy of honor and glory! In the name of Jesus I pray, Amen.

The will to obey God increases the more we experience God's love at work in our lives. To know God's love is to know that God will never lead us to activity that will bring us any type of harm. Lord, we trust you to lead us into greater avenues of ministry and into a healthier relationship with you. In Jesus' name we pray, Amen.

"Lord, may I never get so busy with my own affairs that I fail to respond to the needs of Your people." I pray for the strength to work, the wisdom to produce and a heart to trust in You Holy Spirit.

I am aware that opportunities will often present themselves to reveal things about my mindset, attitude and character. When these times occur, help me to adjust my perception so that I can walk in spiritual understanding. I desire to take advantage of every opportunity that will result in truth and clarity. In Jesus' name I pray, Amen.

◊

I rejoice in the day that you have made and actively seek your wisdom. Lord, I pray that your angels will guard and protect me as your directions for the day are revealed. I declare divine appointments, encounters and exchanges in Jesus' name. Nothing that I connect with today will be by chance because every step I take has been ordered by you. Not one enemy will triumph over me, my family, pastors or friends. You, Oh Lord, are with me; therefore, I will see supernatural turnarounds and miraculous breakthroughs, in Jesus' name. So shall it be!

I intentionally and on purpose bless You with the first fruit of my praise. I believe today that ALL things will work for my good. My spirit is at peace. I pray and welcome the leading of You Holy Spirit. I decree and declare victory over my entire family and all those I love. As I rise, let my feet walk in purpose, and my praise become contagious, in Jesus Name.

I take authority and speak to every element, plan and purpose for this day: "You shall cooperate and fall in line in the name of Jesus. Everything in my space will line up and give God the glory that's due His name!"

◊

Thank you for the dawning of this new day. Cover us with the Blood of Jesus. Take control of the airways that nothing spoken today will be miscommunicated, misdirected or misunderstood. On this day, speak wisdom in our hearing. Unstop clogged ears and hearts that we may hear you clearly, concisely and with clarity. Thank You for keeping my family, pastors and those I love safe from every snare, trap, hole and ditch that the enemy has set. Every step we take will be unhindered because our steps are guarded by angels that have been given charge over us, to keep us in all our ways, lest we dash our foot upon stones. We give you glorious praise! In Jesus' name we pray, AMEN.

◊

Lord, thank you for watching over my life. You have kept me and those I love from dangers seen and unseen. You have protected us from the schemes of the enemy and the snares of the evil one. Position my heart to be alert and cause my ears to be sensitive as I keep my hands lifted towards you. I pray for those who are sick, hurt, wounded, lost, desolate and confused. Heal them like only you can. Send help from unexpected places. I pray for the peace of

Jerusalem. I hold fast to the notion of "everything better"! In the mighty name of Jesus I pray, Amen.

◊

God, I render thanks to you for another day. Please keep me safely under the shadow of your wings. I do not know what today will bring but you know the way. Dispatch your angels to protect my family, friends, coworkers, pastors and leadership, in the name of Jesus. Preserve me for your glory and make me an instrument of your peace. May my life return to you the glory that is due your name!

◊

How awesome is Your Presence! Lord, keep me lifted that I may have words of encouragement for others. I pray for those who are lost and can't find their way. I pray for those who are misjudged, misunderstood and misguided. Keep watch over my ears, heart, thoughts and my imagination. Let every person you have positioned to bless me to release them now, in Jesus' name. Even as I receive, let me also be a blessing. I command all wickedness targeted toward me, my family, pastors and friends, to be bound, in Jesus' name. Release over us the oil of favor, might and power as we bless and glorify your name.

◊

Father, today I look to you and give you praise for another day. Thank You for covering the lives of my family, pastors, and friends. Thank you for your loving kindness and tender care for me. My hands are lifted and my heart is set to bring you glory. Thank you for the mind to meet every task, keep every appointment and handle every assignment. I will not waver in my praise toward you. I bless you with all I have because you've made my heart glad.

◊

Today will be a phenomenal day because you are with me. Before you formed me in my mother's womb, you knew me. You fashioned me for greatness and daily clothe me in your power. I fully trust and believe that my words are powerful and will be used to heal, uplift and edify your people. I WILL open my lips and my mouth WILL declare your praise.

◊

LORD, we praise you for intercepting every plan and plot of the enemy today. Thank you for holding us up as we give glory to your name. Thank you for success in all that we do and say. As declared in Joshua 1:9, we will be strong, courageous, unafraid and encouraged. Thank you for being with us wherever we go.

◊

LORD, hear my voice as I lay my requests before you. My soul longs to hear your voice and heed your commands. Thank you for this time to be with you. I set aside every distraction as I embrace this encounter with you. I trust in your mercy, rely on your love and stand in your strength.

Help me to walk in your truth and not rely on my feelings. Cause me to embrace everything that comes my way as an opportunity to see you at work in my life. Great is your mercy toward me!

◊

God, your name is great! Today my ears are open to hear and my heart is available to be filled. I pray for the protection of my family, pastors and friends. Thank you in advance for keeping us in safety of your wings. I bind every demon that would try to creep in to distract, destroy and deter your people from reaching their destiny. Dispatch angels to guard and protect your people. I pray that every thought and deed be done with a clean heart and with pure intentions. Thank you for full restitution as we release the burden associated with bitterness, failure and missed opportunities. You alone can realign what was misaligned and restore everything that was lost, stolen or given away. Thank you for moving in, through and all around us. In the name of Jesus we pray, Amen.

◊

Holy Spirit, have your way in my life today. I pray that the atmosphere over my family, church and workplace are free and productive. There will be no hold ups, no setbacks and no mishaps, in Jesus' name. I pray for protection from every false accusation, judgmental spirit, and misguided motive. Guard me from discouragement and every ounce of sabotage created by the enemy. Bless me that I will be a blessing to uplift and encourage others. Allow my words to be more than motivation, may they carry life and destroy death, in Jesus' name. Amen.

◊

I command the winds of the earth to take hold of my praise. Cover those that are in need of healing, deliverance, comforting and love. Let my decisions glorify You, my conversations and actions please You. Keep watch over me Lord in my safe place of peace.

Lord, there is no question that you are working on my behalf. I praise you because I can sense the enlarging of my territory and the prosperity of my dwelling place. My "*due*" season has been established in the realm of heaven and is being manifested in the earth. There is no doubt in my mind that this is my time! Every divine appointment and intervention will be accomplished and received today with gratefulness and thanksgiving. I declare that on this day I will live to see the goodness of the Lord in the land of the living! In the matchless name of Jesus I pray, Amen.

Father, we need you. We stand in your name as we come against every demon that has been assigned to burden your people with anxiety attacks, nervous breakdowns, suicide attempts, strokes, heart attacks, heart failure, cancer, loneliness, depression and financial difficulties. We are fully aware that the Blood of JESUS prevails and the name of the Lord is magnified! We give you glory, Lord, as you release the spirit of healing, peace and provision to all who call upon Your name!

◊

I honor You Lord with my best praise. Thank You for being the fortress where I am safe. You are my deliverer, I take refuge in You. Thank You for being the shield of protection over me, my family and all those I love. I declare that You alone are worthy. Thank You for the supernatural windfall of healing, divine debt cancellation and overflowing finances. Here's my praise, make it Your dwelling place, in Jesus name.

◊

Lord, thank you for this moment in time. It is my prayer that your love is evident in me today. I desire to follow you closely and serve as a conduit to draw others to you. Direct my steps as I follow you. Cause me to be a responsible caregiver without worrying about earthly compensation. Fill this day with the kind of peace that surpasses all understanding and guide my heart with your word. Thank you for being the head of my life and the lover of my soul.

Lord, I believe that you will cause all things to fall into place as you grant me favor, influence, and connections. I decree and declare that every dream, promise and goal that you have put in my heart will come to pass, in Jesus' name. So shall it be!

◊

Lord, we pray that as we grow in our worship, you would clean our hands, forgive our sins and wash our hearts. Draw us closer to you and further away from the wiles of the devil. Keep us and we shall be kept! Comfort us and we shall be comforted! There is no doubt that you are the God of great peace, consolation and joy. For this alone, we love, adore and give you the highest praise. Hallelujah!

◊

Thanks you Lord for allowing me to see another day! I am grateful that I woke up in time and not into eternity. Despite the challenges I have faced, I am still here! Today I declare that there are great opportunities awaiting me and blessings with my name on them. I do not take lightly who you created me to be, therefore, I have set my intention on the awesome and amazing things to come. I am determined to keep pushing towards the mark of the high calling in Christ Jesus.

Holy Spirit, I completely depend on you to lead and guide me. Lord, my faith has not always been in you because of the distractions of this world; however, my heart is grateful that you didn't give up on me. All glory and honor belongs to you! I implore your hand to stay upon me and your ears to remain open to my cries. Light my path, order my steps and open doors that I may walk through victoriously. I beg for more of you, in Jesus' name. Amen.

◊

Today I walk in joy and great freedom. In my pursuit of You, thank You for peace of mind. I am content to drink from the overflow of Your presence. Your Good News has changed everything about my life. I praise You for being a constant spring of life-giving water that satisfies. Through it all, I've learned to trust You Holy Spirit. I am absolutely convinced that the best and happiest future imaginable is headed my way. Thank You almighty God for the love You have poured out on the lives of my family, pastors and friends. And for this I give You praise.

Won't He Do it.com

Holy Spirit, please guide my day that I may be strategically lined up with your will. I am contagiously blessed; therefore, every place I walk into today will be blessed as well! I summons your glory to hover over my family, my pastors and friends. Grant us supernatural outpourings and manifested turnarounds, in Jesus name. Amen.

I will NOT live a defeated life. The obstacles I've already endured have made me stronger, wiser and better, in JESUS' name. I am a more than a conquer. I WILL WIN!

◊

Lord, please give your ear unto my petition this morning. I call upon you because only you can help. Take full authority of my day and cleanse my space of all demonic oppression, evil forces and rulers of this world. Trip up every force that would attempt to illegitimately capture my destiny and bind the hand of every strongman whose aim is to thwart your plan for my life. Save me, Oh Lord, and deliver me from the snare of my enemies.

◊

Oh Lord, our Lord, how excellent is your name! I pray that this day is filled with revelation, healing, deliverance, salvation, peace, joy, healthy relationships and financial freedom. I am blessed because of you! Every place that my feet shall tread will become sanctuaries of your glory. Reveal your power and fall on me. In the name of Jesus I pray, Amen.

◊

In the Name of Jesus, I command this morning to take hold of the ends of the earth and shake off the reigns of wickedness that will try to hinder my family, friends and co-workers. I DECREE and DECLARE that today I will have dominion over the enemy and his schemes. Lord, I praise you because you have already won the victory. I appreciate your loving kindness, delight in your tender mercies and bask in the beauty of your holiness.

◊

Holy Spirit, I welcome you to break forth and reveal your purpose for my life today. Thank You for hearing my prayer, in the name of Jesus. Amen.

◊

Lord, I command my day to fully cooperate with your plan and purpose. I greet today with the anticipation of good things, great reports and the divine connections that you have already prepared for me. My hands are lifted and my heart is glad.

◊

Dear Lord, thank you for very this moment in time where I am able to give you praise. On this day increase my energy, decrease my enemies, eliminate emergencies, anoint my efforts & enlarge my income! In the mighty name of Jesus, AMEN!

◊

This is the day you have made and everything in me will rejoice! I celebrate your works, marvel at your miracles and embrace your presence. I pray that the Blood of Jesus will cover and protect my family, friends and associates. Keep us in great health, save us from ourselves and continuously deliver us from evil. Amen.

◊

Father, give us a deeper hunger to walk in your will and submit to your way. Cause our appetites to only desire the meat of your Word. Let us eat from your table that our hearts may be full. We are delighted as you reveal more of who you are and what you have purposed us to be. Fill us with your glory and make your presence known. This is our prayer, Amen.

◊

God, please shut down every ounce of doubt and unbelief within me. Despite the happenings of this day, I will sing and proclaim your name from the depths of my being. You are my strength and my song! You are my inner peace and my joy. Indeed, you are my hope.

◊

Our eyes are upon You O'Lord. We honor You. You have made us to be free, victors, the called, anointed, appointed and empowered. As we abide with You Holy Spirit, we seek Your wisdom and directions for today. We walk in what You have called us to be Holy, a chosen generation, and we rest in knowing You are with us, in Jesus name.

Lord I pray that all my days will be well and multiplied as the days of heaven are upon the earth. I see explosive blessings resting at my door. A sudden widespread of favor will overtake me, my family, pastors and friends because we have obeyed You. Not one window of Your divine healing, supernatural increase and overcoming peace will be missed. Holy Spirit as You lead, put me in the direct path of those assigned to bless me. I command the north, south, east and west, give it up. I will receive with no delay. And it is so, in Jesus name.

◊

Lord thank You for another day. Thank You Holy Spirit for causing me to be in the direct lineup to be blessed. My spirit agrees and anticipates this season of open doors. I abide on course and will not be led astray. I live in the rhema, and it has caused signs, wonders and miracles to be manifested all around me. The Lord has commanded and charged His Angels to guard carefully my family, pastors, and friends as we journey to destiny. LORD, Your name alone is exalted, Your glory is above earth and upon the heaven and among Your people, thank God I'm in it, in Jesus name.

◊

Father, I shut down every doubtful and unbelieving voice within me. I will proclaim that You are Lord from the depths of my being, until I am undergirded and surrounded by Your strength and Your peace. You are my song in the midst of it all. I declare and speak over every element and plan that make up the purpose for my today, you shall cooperate and line up, in Jesus name.

◊

In the midst of all that's going on, I give You my best praise. Yes, there are times when my mind and body don't agree on my praise, so I command my hands to lift and bless You, my lips to magnify Your name out loud, and my heart to rhythmically beat to sic with Yours. I command this day to applaud, salute and honor You. This is the day that You have made, I WILL rejoice and be GLAD in it. Let my actions, deeds, and conversations glorify You. In my heart, I pray for my family, pastors and friends. Let this day be abundantly kind to them, for You alone Lord are worthy of our praise, in Jesus name.

◊

Lord I speak into the hearing of Your people. I pray that Your angels will cover us from every deceptive, diabolical scheme of the enemy to up root, upheave and destroy our peace. I plead the blood of Jesus. Lord we see Your mighty hand at work. Thank You for the protective hedge that surrounds our families, pastors and friends. Let the words of my mouth and the meditation of my heart be acceptable in Your sight. You are our strength and You are our redeemer, in Jesus name. Amen.

I may not understand all right now, but I do know it's all working for my good. Lord, in advance, thank You for my even place of stability. Thank You for covering and ordering my steps as I walk out the plan You have prepared. Let me not forget that You are the author and finisher of my faith. I praise You for my Angels on assignment who do my bidding in Your presence. Great are You Lord. Be glorified in this temple as I usher my praise towards Your Holy place. Holy Spirit, have Your way as I open my heart and ears to You. Bless my family, my pastors and my friends. Keep them safe and under Your protective shield. Mighty are the works of Your hands.

◊

Lord let me greet this day in peace. I pray that in all things I will rely upon Your will. Bless my dealings with all who surround me. In my deeds and words, guide my thoughts and feelings. Let me not forget that You are with me. Holy Spirit teach me to act wisely. Strengthen my hands to accomplish my assignments. I pray and cover my family, pastors and friends. May good success meet them wherever they go. My praise is directed to You, in Jesus name.

◊

I decree and declare, this is the season of opened doors for me and all those I love. Favor is all around me. Everywhere I go today has been instructed to cooperate with the spoken word over my life. There is nothing missing, nothing broken and nothing lacking. I speak to every deliberate wicked seed that the enemy tries plants will produce CROP FAILURE, in Jesus name. My praise has already gone out before me, and my atmosphere is charged, I see victory all around me.

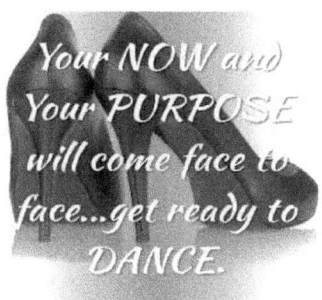

Your NOW and Your PURPOSE will come face to face...get ready to DANCE.

Lord Your Hand is everywhere. Let Your kingdom come and Your will be done. I take delight in You. Thank You for Your love, peace and protection that completely surrounds my family, pastors, leadership and friends. I pray that my thoughts and words are seasoned with grace, as You accelerate my life in fulfilling Your purpose, I return all the glory to You, in Jesus name.

◊

A new day has dawned, and I sense the anointing of the overcomer. Good morning Holy Spirit. I pray that this day will produce unmerited favor for my family, pastors, leadership and friends. I speak to every wicked thing that spent the night making plans to pull me down, I declare I will not be tripped up, entrapped, coerced or pulled out of alignment. I have been positioned ready and I will finish my assignments. My angels on assignment cover the aim of this prayer, in Jesus name.

◊

I acknowledge You Holy Spirit. Thank You for the wisdom to maneuver through circumstances and situations. By faith I believe there will be a demonstration of Your glory. May the seeds of my praise inherit a double portion of Your grace, good health and abundance. I humbly pray for my family, pastors and friends, Lord do it for Your glory. I declare success, victory, and destiny blessings to all who read and believe this prayer, in Jesus name.

◊

Good morning Holy Spirit. As I make my way into this day, disturb me if I lose my thirst for more of You. Disturb me if I sway from Your excellence. Disturb me if I fall short of the goals You have already provided for me to complete. I pray that You will saturate and cover my pastors, family and friends with Your loving kindness and protection. Most of all today, thank You for being the remedy, I'm listening, in Jesus name.

◊

Holy Spirit, I delight myself in You. I lift my hands because I am confident that You hear me. I am in expectation that my family, pastors and friends will walk divinely in Your victory, favor and love. Let the words of my mouth, and the meditation of my heart, be acceptable, in Jesus name!

◊

Good morning Holy Spirit. I don't know the names of everyone here on FB, but You do! I believe a praise has been assigned to every demon, anxiety attacks, nervous breakdowns, suicide attempts, strokes, diabetes, heart attacks, cancer, loneliness, depression and financial difficulties, I glorify You. I pray and believe that supernatural healing, peace and unlimited provisions will be released to all who read this post. I'm gonna put a praise on it at watch it TURN TURN TURN around, in Jesus name.

◊

Good morning Holy Spirit, I am thankful that I can hear You. I pray that my praise will keep me from evil so that my spirit will not be pushed out of alignment. I am on course and on purpose. With my prayer I cover my family, pastors and friends. I praise You that there will be nothing missing, nothing broken and nothing lacking in what my praise is aiming for, total victory, in Jesus name.

◊

Lord, as I lift up my first fruit of praise, You've been good to me. May the life I live point to You, and speak of Your transforming power. Thank You for causing me to succeed with favor. I agree and declare that every dream You have given me will come to pass and I will see it. Thank You for my family, pastors and friends. With You Lord, NOTHING is impossible, in Jesus name.

◊

I command the winds of the earth to take hold of this praise, Lord I just want to thank You. Cover those in need of healing, deliverance, comfort and love. I declare every wicked thing set up to trip, trap and sabotage me is bound and will bow in the presence of You Lord. I speak miracles and blessings into the hearing of everyone I will meet, in Jesus name.

◊

I choose to speak and believe the Word that will shift me into divine alignment. I will prosper. I am confident that You Lord hear me. I am in expectation that I will experience Your victory. Let the words of my mouth and the meditation of my heart line up and BE acceptable to You, in Jesus Name.

◊

I believe His Word and that divine order will manifest. I speak God's Word over my family, pastors and friends. I will keep speaking until I see what I believe. I AFFIRM NOW everything I need His hands have already provided. At the precise time, I will be contacted and contracted by the right person(s) who have what I need to fulfill destiny's call on my life. Lord cover the aim of my prayer, in Jesus name.

As the morning unfolds, thank You. I have no doubt that Your goodness and mercy have my back (Ps. 23:6). I am in divine alignment, and on purpose as I walk in agreement with Your will. I am breaking out on every side and declare I have room to live (Is. 49:20)! I have not missed my opportunity to soar. I am on time, in the right position and surrounded by the right people. My hands are lifted as I give this praise to You, in Jesus name.

◊

I take the mind of Christ as my thoughts for today. I am thankful and rejoicing in everything knowing that "this is the will of God in Christ Jesus concerning me." Lord I thank You for my life.

◊

Thank You for swift, sudden turnarounds. Hallelujah!! I pray for those in need of divine healing, deliverance, comforting and love. I declare VICTORY over every scheme, plot and plan the enemy sent to detour my praise. May Your abundant peace be the fence around my family, pastors and friends. Keep a watch over my ears, heart, thoughts, and imagination. I will bless You with my praise, in Jesus name.

◊

I will not let my mouth betray my expectation. I declare, I am contagiously blessed. I speak exuberant healing, peace and abundance over my family, pastors and friends. I pray that the fresh oil of favor will saturate every step I take, as I deliberately bless You Lord with my best praise, in Jesus name.

◊

In my pursuit of You, thank You for peace of mind. I praise You for being a constant spring of life-giving water that satisfies. Through it all, I'm trusting in You Holy Spirit. Thank You almighty God for the love You have poured out on the lives of my family, pastors and friends. For this I give You praise.

◊

Let God arise and His enemies be scattered. Good morning Holy Spirit. I declare today every adversity you face, will drop, unfold and unwrapped victory all in your favor. Maintain on course, your VICTORY is at hand. Stand up, it's absolutely working for your good.

◊

You whispered my name and immediately my spirit arose to greet You. Good morning Holy Spirit. I receive Your Word for success, prosperity, health, wealth, vision, direction, ingenuity, creativity, spirituality, holiness and righteousness. You have put me on an accelerated path as I put my trust in You. I praise and apply Your Word all over my life, my family and my job. I am an overcomer and I do it with exceeding joy, in Jesus Name.

Your season of suddenly will cause the enemy to drop his jaw. There is monumental favor, influence, and divine connections accessing the atmosphere of your praise, Hallelujah!! I agree with you and declare that every dream, every promise, and every set goal are coming to pass, in Jesus name.

INSPIRATIONAL THOUGHTS

> SPEAK what you SEEK until you SEE what you've SAID.
> - unknown

What if your next praise SHIFTED you to that next level and you receive the word YOU HAVE THE JOB; Doctor calls, all the way HEALED; bank makes a mistake, KEEP the money; multiple bills paid in FULL; released from a secret bondage you dare not expose, but you told Jesus, RECONCILED; Family matter TAKEN CARE of; addicted family member or friend "DELIVEREDDDDDDDD". Now put a PRAISE on that!

But You, O'Lord, are forever exalted.

Faith is motion not emotions.

You can't stress over what God has already given you clarity on.

What you thought would come as a thunder, came in as a whisper. What you thought would come as the end, came as the beginning, all because you trusted in Him.

Everyone will not be included in your NEXT CHAPTER. It's ok. Who will be there will absolutely blow your mind. A God-moment.

Prayer is not asking. It is putting yourself in the hands of God, at His disposition, and listening to His voice in the depth of our hearts.

Pick up your pace, God's favor is on your life. You're on the right track as you trust in this God-moment. I'm headed in a new direction, been that way, I'm going the other way.

In all your travels
In all your work
In all your social life
In all your education
In all your everything - remember this one thing: God is after you.

Your spiritual discernment will keep you safe.

It's been a long time coming, but I know, a change is going to come, Ooohhh yes it is. ~ Sam Cook

When you stay and allow people to constantly keep you in bondage by bringing up your past, it's time for you to move away from the people.

Your destiny is waiting and it's better than you could have ever imagined.

Nothing the enemy does can abort the plan that God has set for your life.

My heart is convinced that on this day, GOD will blow my mind with miracles, signs and wonders.

God is going to do something phenomenal, something substantial and something incredible just for you!!

We must learn to see the hand of God in everything we encounter and rest in the fact that God does all things well!

Always do your best. Whatever you plant now, you will harvest later. Make sure that you have promising seed in the ground.

Too often we underestimate the power associated with a touch, smile, and kind word or listening ear; all of which have the potential to turn someone's day around. Let's be intentional about spreading acts of kindness!

I am LIVING on Purpose and I'm sticking to it!

You are about to experience a sudden miracle that will attract global attention! Your barren tree shall become fruitful, in Jesus' name.

Look for God in every circumstance that comes your way. HE IS Jehovah Jireh, the One who will provide the means to catapult you into destiny. Paul says its best, "And my God shall supply all your needs according to His riches in glory by Christ Jesus." (Phil4:19) Hallelujah!!

Lord I give you all the glory. I have no doubt that it was you that made this moment possible! In you do I live, move and have my being.

It's the battles that produce the victories and the victors! Listen here, "we are hard pressed on every side, but not crushed; perplexed, but not in despair; persecuted, but not abandoned; struck down, but not destroyed" 2 Cor. 4:8, NIV. God will change either your circumstances or He'll change you. Either way, He'll bring you out on top.

"No weapon that has been made to be used against you will succeed. You will have an answer for anyone who accuses you. This is the inheritance of the LORD's servants. Their victory comes from me," declares the LORD." (Isaiah 54:17)

I will lift my voice and sing because your love has done amazing things. I rest in the fact that my life is in Your Hands. "For I know the thoughts that I think toward you, says the Lord, thoughts of peace and not of evil, to give you a future and a hope." (Jeremiah 29:11)

You can never be who you're going to be while being who you used to be. The litmus test for growth is change.

God is able to do just what HE said He would do, He's going to fulfill every promise to you, don't give up on God, cause He won't give up on you, He's ABLE!

Lord, thank you for turning my mess into a miracle.

When God takes you to a new place, you must leave the last place alone.

God can't stop speaking to you because HE is the Word; HE can't stop making a way because HE is the way; HE can't lie because HE is the truth; and what you need Him to do is already done because HE IS.

Dare to grow in your dreams! Put your faith into action while you speak these words, "I BELIEVE that my words are powerful. I BELIEVE I will see everything I've prayed for. I

BELIEVE God will do everything He promised. In the name of Jesus I pray, Amen."

God will bless you in public with what He's promised you in private. That's more than enough reason to give Him praise.

I decree and declare that abundance is coming and it's bringing endless possibilities.

We must continue to walk this journey together in authentic love and forgivenes.

We must listen and be heard. We must encourage and inspire with loving kindness and courage. We must remain faithful to the truth, even if it's not popular. Above all else, we MUST honor God.

Let me encourage you to take some time this week to sit back and enjoy a chat (no text, no email) with someone you haven't been able to connect with in a long time. Listen to their heart, challenge their fears and encourage them to live on purpose!

God has been pursuing you since the beginning of time. In Psalm 63:8, David declares, "My soul follows close behind you; your right hand upholds me." David desired to be intimately acquainted with God and therefore cries out, "OH that I might know Him." May our pursuit of God cause us to conform to His likeness.

Life is an opportunity; benefit from it. Life is a dream; realize it. Life is a challenge; meet it. Life is a duty; complete it. Life is a promise; fulfill it. Life is too precious; do not destroy it. Live your life on purpose and keep moving forward!

Psalm 27:4: "One thing I have desired of the LORD, that I shall seek: That I may dwell in the house of the LORD all the days of my life, to behold the beauty of the LORD, And to inquire in His temple."

May the Lord answer you when you are in distress; may the God of Jacob protect you from despair. May He send you help from the sanctuary and grant you support from Zion. May He remember all your sacrifices and accept your offerings of praise.

I believe that monumental changes will take place in my life that will propel me forward!

Honor God, listen to the Holy Spirit and never waver in your faith. "So then faith comes by hearing, and hearing by the Word of God." (Romans10:17)

"May He give you the desires of your heart and make all your plans succeed. May we shout for joy over your victory and lift up our banners in the name of God, May the Lord grant all your requests." (Psalm 20: 4-5)

There's nobody GREATER than our God!

The DNA results are in and Satan, "YOU ARE NOT THE FATHER!"

Free your mind and the rest will follow. *Galatians 5:1 asserts*, "Stand fast therefore in the liberty by which Christ has made us free, and do not be entangled again with a yoke of bondage."

John 5:14-15 reads, "NOW this is the confidence that we have in Him that if we <u>ask</u> anything according to His will, He hears us."

Even if prayer doesn't change *it*; prayer has the power to change *me*! Engaging in conversation with you makes everything so much easier to bear. Truly your yoke is easy and your burden is light. I rest in the fact that just a little talk with you makes everything right.

A good friend once told me, "Never think yourself out of the thoughts God has toward you." Jeremiah 29:11 "For I know the plans I have for you," DECLARES THE LORD, "plans to prosper you and not to harm you, plans to give you hope and a future." (Emphasis added) God KNOWS you, loves you and plans to prosper you!

"Now unto Him that is able to do exceeding abundantly above all that we ask or think, according to the power that works in us." (Ephesians 3:20)

The enemy does not come after empty vessels; on the contrary, he schemes to steal, kill and destroy those who are striving to enhance their lives for God. The greatest defense against the enemy is to know the truth and allow it to make you free. Strive for truth in your heart, emotions, words, actions and thoughts. As inferred in John 3:21, let all of your deeds be made manifest by operating in truth.

"I beseech *(to beg eagerly for; appeal)* you therefore, brethren, by the mercies of God, that you present your bodies a living sacrifice, holy, acceptable to God, which is your reasonable service. And do not be conformed to this world, but be transformed by the renewing of your mind, that you may prove what is that good and acceptable and perfect will of God."(Romans 12:1) Position yourself to embrace the higher things God has in store for you by the renewing of your mind!

We are surrounded by the One who made us; the One who is I AM. It is imperative that we embrace our identity as children of God and heirs to the throne. Adoption, justification and glorification are all gifts granted by our Father in heaven.

Say this aloud: "I am going to press through this place because I am on my way out. I am being healed from any hurt and pain that has kept me bound. I agree now, in the name of the Lord, that I am free and will forever walk in victory!"

God longs for a relationship with each of us that is marked by the same intimacy David expressed in Psalm 23. Whether we are in the midst of green pastures, beside still waters or in the valley of the shadow of death, God wants to walk with us every day. All we have to do is listen for His voice and follow his leading.

God knows how to turn our sad stories into joyful ones, moments into memories and friends into life savers. Don't get stuck in the down moments of life; God delights in building you back up!

Be a visible blessing to a living God.

I will not lose hope. Things are going to get better. I am coming out of this!

In order to increase your bread for eating, you must increase your seed for sowing.

Envision yourself accomplishing dreams, overcoming obstacles, accepting promotion and remaining healthy, strong, and prosperous. Sometimes, you have to see it before you SEE IT.

Praise Him in the middle of *IT*! God is working it out for you!

I am absolutely convinced that nothing—living or dead, angelic or demonic, high or low, thinkable or unthinkable can come separate me from the love of God through Christ Jesus!

Never lose grip of God's presence in your life. It is an awesome privilege to be in relationship with such a loving God. Allow Him to Lord over your life as you wholeheartedly fight the good fight of faith. No matter the cost, finish your kingdom assignment and declare with the Apostle Paul, "I have finished the course; I have kept the faith" *(2 Timothy 3:7).* Live your life on PURPOSE!

You have no idea who's observing your life today. Every second, minute and hour you have spent restoring, healing, and blessing others will produce a harvest with incredible favor!

Jeremiah 1:12 NIV ~ The LORD said to me, "You have seen correctly, for I am watching to see that MY WORD is fulfilled." God's Word always produces the exact result that He sent it to accomplish. It never returns to Him void, it has to be fulfilled. While we may not know the exact time or date, we do know that His Word shall come to pass. Keep the faith.

Each morning God deposits 1,440 minutes into your day account. You can invest them, but you can't save them. Take a look at yesterday's ledger; it's a prophecy of your future, unless you rise up and take control of your time. Start your today the way you intend to continue it— prayerfully! David said, "In the morning, I lay my requests before you and wait in expectation" (Psalms 5:3, NIV).

Just as you received Christ Jesus as Lord, so walk in Him. Colossians 2:6 ~ The Bible often compares life to a walk, because life is a journey; we're not sitting still. Throughout the New Testament, we are told to walk in wisdom, love, light, and obedience. We're told to walk as Jesus walked. We're also told to walk alongside other people. Here are three reasons to walk with other people: it's safer, it's supportive and it's healthy.

> **Psalm 112:3**
>
> Wealth and riches are in my house & business.

Jesus will work it out if you let Him.

When you are assured of your purpose, you can't be intimidated by your circumstances, because they will all bow to God's purpose for your life.

Don't be influenced by who is sitting next you. GO for what you know, believe you will receive, and you will have it.

You are at a major turning point and something phenomenal is knocking at your door.

Don't breakdown and pass out now, your victory is at hand.

I am convinced that "my next miracle is looking for me" and it will work for my good!!

He blesses commanded work! What's your vision? What has God told you to do? Know your assignments, and refuse to be sidetracked, detoured, or pushed out of alignment by anything less. It's all about the Kingdom y'all.

God always has a VICTORY when you go through.

Little minds have great wishes; great minds have causes. Have you found a purpose great enough to hold you steady in the storm, strong enough to keep you going when everything is against you? Behind every great accomplishment, there's a purpose—not a wish! It's time to break camp, ask God for directions and then move out with confidence.

My heart proclaims the truth that HE is marvelous, better than good, Holy, righteous, incredible, wonderful and phenomenal.

Love HIM with your hands today. Every time you think of HIS goodness towards you, slide those hands up and bless HIM.

Forgive those who've hurt you—including yourself. The issue isn't whether you remember, but how you remember. God is able to take the sting out of all those memories and still leave the sweet taste of victory intact.

Someone is always observing you who is capable of blessing you. That's how the favor of God works—through people. Listen: "Do you see a man who excels in his work? He will stand before kings" (Proverbs 22:29).

Until I see what I believe, I'll keep praising Him on purpose. God is up to something. I feel it!!!

I may not know what to do, but I do know where to look for my eyes are upon Him.

A blessed person doesn't just grow; they are planted in a definite time and place to accomplish a definite purpose. God's not concerned about how high your trunk grows; He's concerned about how deep your roots go, for that determines what you will produce!

When God gives you a vision, you'll be able to look beyond the hardness and see the harvest. You won't just see the ruins, you'll see the rebuilding and He will do something spectacular, He will make you a part of it. Let's get to work.

The way God took you in life was to prepare you for THIS PLACE and TIME.

Our intentions must match our actions.

> When you are going through something hard and wonder where God is, remember the teacher is always quiet during a test.

Don't give God what's left, give what's right; first giving honor to God who is the head of my life, you know the rest ... all the Glory belongs to Him.

I'm a living witness that your past can be a mess, but your future will be amazing. Stay with God.

Whatever you invest in will strengthen you. And because God is your source, your future has already been framed.

And now to Him who can keep you on your feet, standing tall in His bright presence, fresh and celebrating—to our one God, our only Savior, through Jesus Christ, our Master, be glory, majesty, strength, and rule before all time, and now, and to the end of all time. Yes. (Jude 1:24 MSG)

God's not asking you to fill someone else's shoes, He asking you to find your own shoes. He'll be with you every step of the way.

This morning God deposited 1,440 minutes into your day account. You can invest them, but you can't save them. Take a look at yesterday's ledger; it's a prophecy of your future, unless you rise up and take control of your time. Start your today the way you intend to continue it—prayerfully! David said, "In the morning, I lay my requests before you and wait in expectation" (Psalms 5:3, NIV).

Every day there's a "possibility" of a TURNAROUND. I am a miracle waiting to happen.

The next time you find yourself waiting for a stoplight to change, spend that time thanking God for His goodness to you.

God has not changed His mind about you. Every promise He has given you is still "yes and amen." He is leading you to victory.

STARTING A NEW LIFE WITH CHRIST

God loves you and has a plan for you!

The Bible says, "God so loved the world that He gave His one and only Son, [Jesus Christ], that whoever believes in Him shall not perish, but have eternal life." *(John 3:16)*

Jesus said, "I came that they may have life and have it abundantly."—a complete life full of purpose *(John 10:10)*

We have all done thought or said bad things, which the Bible calls "sin." The Bible declares, "All have sinned and fall short of the glory of God" *(Romans 3:23).*

The result of sin is spiritual separation from God, which ultimately leads to death. *(Romans 6:23).*

The Good News

God sent His Son to die for your sins!

Jesus died in our place so we could have a relationship with God and be with Him forever.

"God demonstrates His own love toward us, in that while we were yet sinners, Christ died for us." *(Romans 5:8)*

The story of redemption does not end with His death on the cross. Christ rose again and still lives!

"Christ died for our sins - He was buried - He was raised on the third day, according to the Scriptures." *(1 Corinthians 15:3-4)*

Jesus is the only way to God. Jesus said, "I am the way, and the truth, and the life; no one comes to the Father, but through Me." *(John 14:6)*

Would you like to receive God's forgiveness?

We can't earn salvation; we are saved by God's grace when we have faith in His Son, Jesus Christ. All you have to do is, "Confess with your mouth, the Lord Jesus and believe in your heart that God raised him from the dead, you will be saved."*(Romans 10:9)*

Prayer to accept Christ as your Savior:

"Dear Lord Jesus,

I know I am a sinner, and I ask for your forgiveness. I believe you died for my sins and rose from the dead. Teach me to trust and follow you as my Lord and Savior. Guide my life and help me to do your will. In Jesus' name I pray, Amen."

This book was presented to me by:

_____

Contact Number: (   ) _____

Email Address:

www.ingramcontent.com/pod-product-compliance
Lightning Source LLC
Chambersburg PA
CBHW061303040426
42444CB00010B/2493